L M N O P

and

All the Letters

A to Z

"I've seen many alphabets in my 22 years of teaching, but <u>LMNOP</u> takes it to a new level."
Pola Espinoza, Master Teacher Consultant, Pajaro Unified School District, Watsonville, CA

"My three year old daughter has been learning the rhymes. They're better than Mother Goose!"
Renée Soppet

"We didn't want to turn the page, but we couldn't wait to see what the next letter had to say."
Melanie Pitcher (she, her mother, and her daughter reading <u>LMNOP</u> together)

....

LEMONTREE PRESS
530 Larkin Street
Monterey, California 93940

Copyright © 2000 Howard Schrager and Bruce Bischof
First Printed Edition 1999
Second Printed Edition 2004
Third Printed Edition 2006
Forth Printed Edition 2010
Fifth Printed Edition 2015
ISBN 0-9644846-0-9

Schrager, Howard.
    LMNOP and all the letters A to Z / poems by
Howard Schrager ; illustrations by Bruce Bischof. --
Fourth edition.
        pages cm
        SUMMARY: Twenty-six playful pictures and poems
derived from original stories or borrowed from fairy and
folk tales illuminate the letters of the alphabet for
children.
    Audience: Ages 6-9.
    ISBN 978-0-9644846-0-3
    1.
        Alphabet rhymes. 2. Children's poetry.
[1. Alphabet. 2. American poetry.]   I. Bischof, Bruce,
illustrator. II. Title. III. Title: LMNOP and all the
letters A to Z.

PS3569.C52848L26 2015   811'.6
                    QBI15-600007

L M N O P
and
All the Letters
A to Z

Poems by Howard Schrager
Illustrations by Bruce Bischof

Published by

Lemon Tree Press

DEDICATION

---

*To Waldorf teachers world-wide, and to all teachers and
parents who realize that, through embracing a creative approach to educating
the children in their care, they are shaping a more truly human future.*

ACKNOWLEDGEMENTS

I wish to acknowledge the tremendous contribution of Rudolf Steiner, who had the courage, the clarity and the concern to introduce Waldorf education into the world as a light into the future.

All the Letters
from
A to Z

Ah radiant star
Far, far away,
I have in my heart
A warm place where you stay.
A is in air
The water of lakes
In apple and apricot
Pies that we bake.
Through April and August,
Autumn to May,
We gather the harvest
Of Nature's array.

B is in bowl, bag, basket, and bin,
All manner of places
To keep berries in.
A brawny brown bear
Called Big Belly
Beholds a bee buzzing;
Oh our busy B.

C makes its sound
In circle and center,
In ceiling and cellar,
In city and cement.
C is a cave of crystal
Cleft from a cliff
'Neath a craggy crest.

Daring D goes under the ground
Where the deadly dragon dwells,
To defend the kingdom sore distressed,
And all danger lay to rest.
Then D opens the door
On the light of day
Where D meets a friend
At the end of enD.

Eagle of light
I seek in the heights;
Toward your beam
Now I reach,
As you stream
From the east.
E's in the elbow
I bend when I eat;
E's doubly there
In my knees and my feet;
E's in my eyes,
E's in my head,
E's in my dreams
When I sleep in my bed.

Firebird fly
From the flickering flames;
Ferns unfurl amidst the fog.
F's not just fine,
It's fairly fantastic-
With flowers and fairies and frogs.
Fur, fins, and feathers
Have animal friends;
An elf by himself
Finds an f at the end.

Good golly!
Good gracious!
Oh gee!
A goose in the roots of a tree!
Ghosts and goblins at Halloween;
In summertime
Glowworms glimmer and gleam.
Gather together for games
On the green;
Fantastic gymnastics
Turns glumness to glee!

Hip, hip, hooray!
H is happy to say
Harvests and holidays;
A haystack so high,
A hare hopping by;
Hear the horns blow,
Hi ho here we go!

I is in ice,
In icicle twice,
But I is not cold,
It's like fire in the night.
Few words start with I,
But often you'll find
"i" in the middle of things.
Most of all, it stands straight and tall;
When we speak of ourselves
We say "I".

January, June, July,
Jester jump so high;
Juggle seven jam jars in the air;
Just jingle your bells,
We'll jump for joy!

King Karl kept his kingdom calm.

His cook kept the kitchen clean.

In kick we find K

Both front and back,

But it's just in the back

Of black, jack and sack.

The king was kind to his kin;

The knight was humble,

He knew to kneel.

L is lively, lovely, laughing,
Like leaves and lilies filled with light.
Luscious, loads, lots,
Not only a little.
L is like a well;
No other letter loves us so well.

Misty mountains multiply
A million marvelous M's;
Mingle mint and marigold
In meadows of mystery.
The moon sends down its magic beams
Making merry melodies
On the mirrors of murmuring streams.

N is not now,

Never, nor;

Naughty and nasty are not nice.

Knit a net and knot it,

Nice and neatly done;

Never let your fingers slow;

Nimble fingers knit nine rows.

Now cast your net

As day is dawning,

Into the newness

Of the morning.

One whole world
Oh so round
In a ring
Joyous sound;
Round as a doughnut,
Round as a bowl;
Our lips make this shape
When we pronounce O.

P is Prince Pumpernickel
With his chest all puffed out.
He's proud as a peacock,
Parading about.
Do you prefer peaches to pears or plums?
Potatoes with parsley and peas,
Please have some.
People and places and parties are fun,
But before pillow time,
Pots and pans must be done.

Q is a queen
Who quibbled and quarreled
When anyone questioned
Or when they kept quiet.
A queer little servant
She called 'Little U',
Followed her faithfully
Whatever she'd do.
She stuck fast in a quagmire
Being quite stout;
There she quivered and quaked
Till he quick pulled her out.

R is in river
Beginning to end,
As it roars through the rapids
And runs 'round the bend.
R is a rough and ragged rascal
Racing and rollicking 'round the block.
R is ready to str-r-retch like rubber,
Or remain rigid as rock.

Swirling stars on a summer night

Shimmer and sparkle before our sight.

Swallows and swifts,

Sparrows and sylphs

Swoop and swerve

In spectacular curves.

S is the snake

That slithers through the grass.

Watch the smoke swirl,

Out the chimney it passes.

The truth of T is plain to see;

It's no tall tale or fantasy;

T's tall and straight from bottom to top,

Like a tower with a turret on top.

Tuesday and Thursday,

Two days of the week.

Tell us the time-

Thanks, it's ten twenty-three.

Our tongue's at our teeth

When we pronounce T.

T must be true,

That's the way T must be.

Universe so wide and blue,
You are too beautiful, too huge.
Beyond the ocean, beyond the moon
What is there you don't include?
The planets turn a whirling tune
Jupiter, Saturn and Neptune.
U may make you upset, unhappy, confused,
Put you under the weather, unusually blue.
If the Ugly Urf is disturbing you,
The Unicorn urges you,
Utterly do!

Valley so vast
With violet vines,
You climb up to a village
Volcanoes behind.
A voice rings out
Filled with vigor and vim,
Venture to vanquish
Be valiant, my friend.
The vile villain
With the velvet vest
Will vanish by evening-
Your victory's met.

Wonders of the world,
Winds that wail and whisper,
Waves that wash the shore,
Wings that soar,
Women weaving,
Willows weeping,
Wish and work,
Water and wine,
Who, what, where, when, why?

X beginning a word
Is exceedingly rare,
Xylophone and x-ray
To name just a pair.
Next let me explain
For example you see
Excessive excuses to His Excellency.
A very fine place to put this cross
Is at the end of such words
As ax, ox, and fox.

Yellow bird in yon yew tree
You sing a lovely melody.
Y is in yarrow and yolk and young,
Year, yawn, and yesterday.
The middle of eye,
The end of why,
The end of many words we spy.
And if you haven't guessed,
Y-E-S spells yes.

Zig-zags of lightning
Zeus hurls through the skies,
Amazing and dazzling
Our wonder-filled eyes.
Lazy zebras at the zoo
Doze on hazy summer days.
The crazy pattern of their suits
Is just the thing that makes them cute.
Zebediah, Zebulon, Zachary,
Zanzibar and Zambezi.

Other Works by Howard Schrager
&

Lemon Tree Press

Available Now:

LMNOP Alphabet Wall Cards

Working With LMNOP, A Manual for Parents and Teachers

King Maximo and the Number Knights

Sarah and the Number Knights

Multiplicando

A Knife and a Fork and a Bottle and a Cork

Chicken in the Car and the Car Can't Go!

Rock Forms Poem (Poster)

Song of the Rain-Poem of California's Water Cycle (Poster)

LemonTree Press, 530 Larkin Street,
Monterey, California 93940
howardschrager@lmntreepress.com

www.lmntreepress.com

Working with LMNOP and All the Letters A to Z

A companion manual to *LMNOP and All the Letters A to Z*, for Parents and Teachers.

Stories, Poetry, Music, Movement, Speech, Drama, and Drawing and other activities cultivate a context out of which children may receive an artistic grounding in language.

"Academics" are not shunned, but are brought within the circuit of this *imaginative field*.

Praise for *Working with LMNOP and All the Letters A to Z*

"One of the best curriculum guides I've ever seen, in it you will find the most creative, energetic, enthusiastic, wise and do-able lesson plan suggestions for each and every letter! The author suggests a story for each letter that relates to the images in LMNOP; he goes on to suggest a delightful list of activities that build a variety of skills."
-Nancy Parsons-

Lemon Tree Press

www.lmntreepress.com

Singing LMNOP

Melodies lend wings to the LMNOP verses. *Singing LMNOP,* presents letter verses in musical form. Children will be quick to learn these simple melodies by heart.

Available as a digital download from our website www.lmntreepress.com.

LMNOP Laminated Prints

"A Children's Poetic Art Gallery of the Alphabet".

LMNOP and All the Letters A to Z is also available as a set of twenty-six 8 1/2×11 laminated cards.

The free standing laminated cards have pictures on one side, verses on the other.

L is lively, lovely laughing,
Like leaves and lilies filled with light.
Luscious, loads, lots,
Not only a little.
L is like a well;
No other letter loves us so well.

B is in bowl, bag, basket, and bin,
All manner of places
To keep berries in.
A brawny brown bear
Called Big Belly
Beholds a bee
Buzzing,
Oh our busy bee.

Valley so vast
With violet vines,
You climb up to a village
Volcanoes behind.
A voice rings out
Filled with vigor and vim,
Venture to vanquish
Be valiant, my friend.
The vile villain
With the velvet vest
Will vanish by evening -
Your victory's met.

Lemon Tree Press